Johann Sebastian Bach

Johann Sebastian Bach was born at Eisenach in Thuringia, Germany, on March 2. The same year saw the birth of the great Domenico Scarlatti as well as the renow... George Frideric Handel. J. S. Bach was a descendant of a long line of musicians. In Germany during that time, the name "Bach" had become almost synonymous with "musician."

Bach's parents died when he was only 10 years old. He was raised by his oldest brother, who was very jealous of Johann Sebastian's superior musical talents. He would not let the youngster use a musical book that he owned, which was filled with great compositions of master composers. The young Bach was able to get his hands on the book at night, however, by slipping it through the lattice-work doors of the bookcase in which it was locked. He copied it all by moonlight and damaged his eyesight permanently in doing so. When he discovered what the boy had done, the older brother took the copy away from him, but to no avail, since Johann Sebastian had already memorized the entire book!

At age 15, when his older brother died, Johann Sebastian became a choir boy at the school of St. Michael, in Luneberg, 200 miles away. In this new setting he was able to diligently study music and improve himself as a performer and composer.

At the age of 19 he accepted his first professional job as an organist, in a church at Arnstadt. Four years later he became the organist at Mulhausen, where he married his cousin, Maria Barbara.

Bach's musical genius reached its greatest heights at Leipzig, Germany, where he was appointed cantor at the St. Thomas School, with responsibility for all the musical activities of its associated churches. In 1720 Maria Barbara died, and a year later Bach married Anna Magdalena Wilcken, a young singer who became a loving mother to Bach's family of 7 children, and bore him 13 more.

Bach's phenomenal output as a composer includes enough music to fill 46 volumes the size of an encyclopedia. He wrote hundreds of keyboard works, including music for clavichord, harpsichord and organ, as well as solos for violin, cello and other instruments. He also composed numerous instrumental duets, trios and orchestral works, and more than 250 sacred and secular cantatas. But the quality of his compositions is even more remarkable than the great quantity. No one has ever written greater music, particularly in the contrapuntal style, and Johann Sebastian Bach ranks as one of the towering musical geniuses of all time.

In 1725 Bach presented his wife, Anna Magdalena, with a beautiful notebook as a birthday present. In this book, Anna Magdalena, Johann Sebastian and other members of the family wrote many short and easy pieces that were either composed by Bach or were favorite pieces of the family. These are the simplest pieces we have from the family circle, and some of these are included on the following pages. In these pieces, there are often repeats of each half. It is customary to embellish (add trills, etc.) on the repeats as heard on the recording.

After a long and prolific career, Bach died in Leipzig, Germany on July 28, 1750.

Signs, Symbols and Terms

Roman Numerals

I 1	IV 4	VII 7	X 10
II 2	V 5	VIII 8	XI 11
III 3	VI 6	IX 9	XII 12

adagio = A slow tempo which is faster than *largo* and slower than *andante*.

allegro = Cheerful, quick or fast.

allegretto = A lively quick tempo that moves more slowly than *allegro*.

andante = A moderate, graceful tempo, slower than *allegretto* and faster than *adagio*.

a tempo = Return to the original tempo.

cantabile = Singing.

commodo = Comfortable, leisurely.

con brio = With vigor.

con moto = With motion.

cresc. = Abbreviation for *crescendo*. Gradually becoming louder.

D.C. al Fine = *Da capo al fine.* Go back to the beginning of the piece and play to the *Fine*, which is the end of the piece.

dim. = Abbreviation for *diminuendo*. Gradually becoming softer.

dolce = Sweet.

gliss. = Abbreviation for *glissando*. To slide from one note to another. Often shown as a diagonal line with an S (slide) in guitar music.

harm. = Abbreviation for *harmonic*. Notes of the harmonic series that are very pure and clear. In this book, written at the sounding pitch with a diamond shaped note head. Touch the string lightly directly over the indicated fret and pluck, immediately removing the finger from the string.

largo = Very slow and broad.

legato = Smooth, connected.

leggiero = Light or delicate.

BV₃ = Barre three strings at the 5th fret.

BV = Barre all six strings at the 5th fret.

HBV = Hinge barre at the 5th fret. Play an individual note on the 1st string with the bottom of the 1st finger, just above the palm. Usually simplifies the next fingering.

⑥ **= D =** Tune the 6th string down to D

p, i, m, a = The right-hand fingers starting with the thumb.

1, 2, 3, 4, 0 = The left-hand fingers starting with the index finger, and the open string.

> = *Accent*. Emphasize the note.

= *Arpeggiate*. Quickly "roll" the chord.

∧ = *Marcato*. Emphasize more than an accent.

l.v. = Abbreviation for *laissez vibre* (let vibrate).

maestoso = Sublime or magnificent.

moderato = In a moderate tempo.

molto = Very or much.

non troppo = But not too much so.

più = More.

poco a poco = Little by little.

rall. = Abbreviation for *rallentando*. Becoming gradually slower.

rit. = Abbreviation for *ritardando*. Becoming gradually slower.

sempre = Always.

sostenuto = Sustained.

staccato = Short, detached.

tranquillo = Tranquil, calm, quiet.

vivace = Lively, quick.

Reading Tablature

Tablature is a purely graphic way of showing what to play on the guitar. There are six lines, each representing one of the strings. Numbers placed on the lines indicate what fret to play on that string.

In this book, the tablature is always written parallel to the standard notation, which already contains all the rhythmic information, so the tablature only indicates the fret numbers and strings.

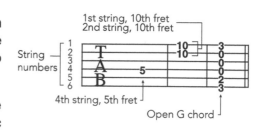

J.S. Bach

Guitar **TAB** *Classics*

16 well-known pieces by one of the world's greatest composers, arranged for guitar

ONLINE ACCESS INCLUDED

Stream or download the audio content for this book.
To access, visit: **alfred.com/redeem**
Enter the following code: 00-22627_553322

Table of Contents

🔊 **Track 1** There is a recording included with this book. It includes performances of all the pieces. Use it to help insure that you are interpreting the rhythms correctly and capturing the style of each work. This symbol will appear to the left of each piece. The track numbers correspond to the piece you want to hear. Track 1 will help you tune to the recording. Enjoy!

Trio to a Menuet

Track 2

Menuet in G

from Anna Magdalena's Notebook

 Track 3

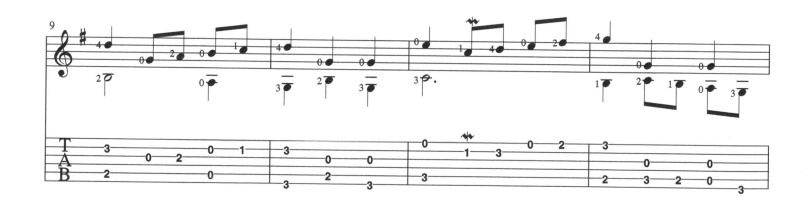

* ꙮ = *Inverted mordent.* Quickly pull-off to a the *lower neighbor* (B) and then hammer-on to the C.

* ⌁ = *Mordent*. Quickly hammer-on to the *upper neighbor* (C) and then pull-off to the B. Or, perform a *trill* (start on the C and quickly pull-off/hammer-on several times, ending on the B).

Menuet in A Minor

from *Anna Magdalena's Notebook*

 Track 4

March

from *Anna Magdalena's Notebook*

 Track 5

* *tr* = *Trill.* Start on the upper neighbor (C-sharp) and quickly pull-off/hammer-on several times, ending on the B.

Musette

from *Anna Magdalena's Notebook*

Track 6

Jesu, Joy of Man's Desiring

 Track 7

Prelude
from *Cello Suite No. 1*

 Track 8

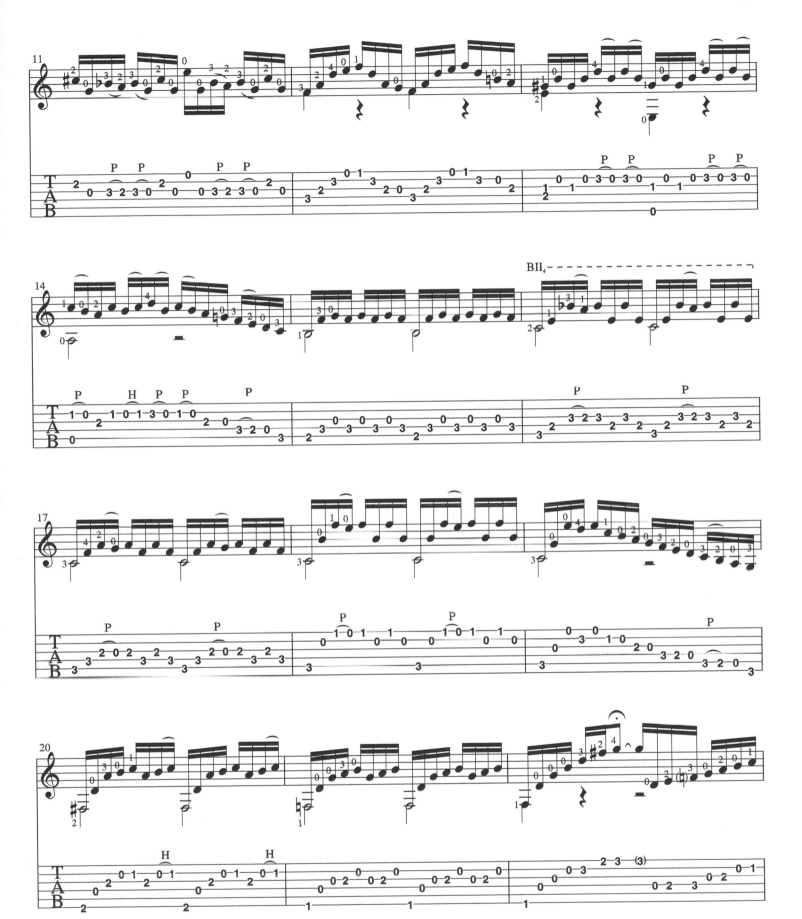

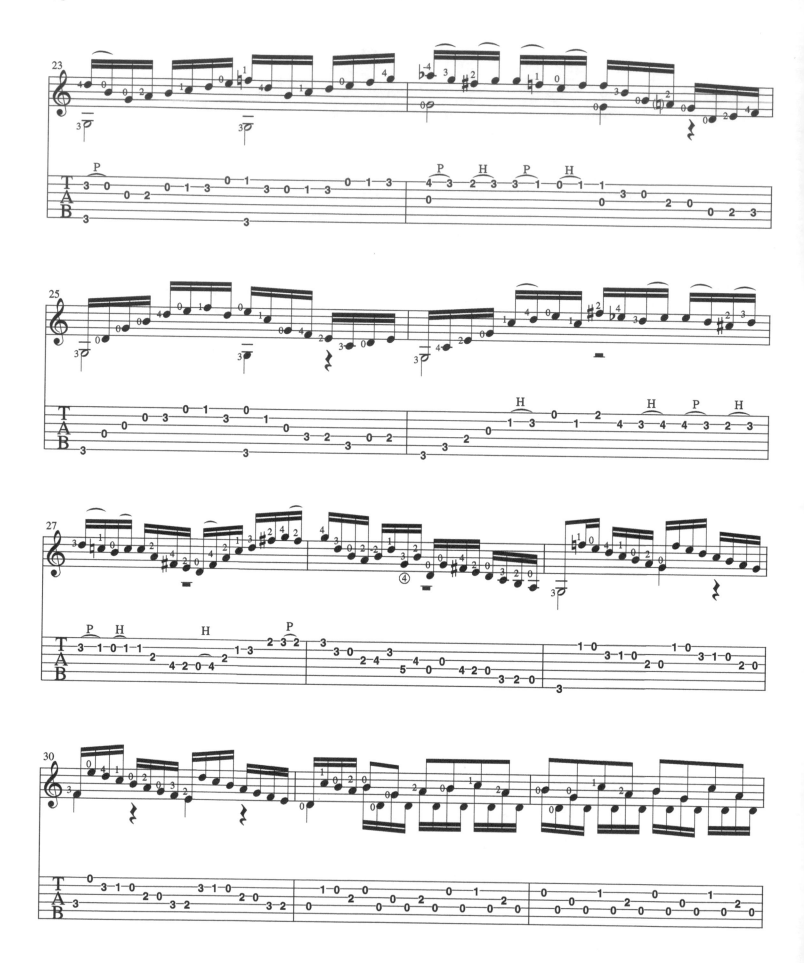

Menuet

Track 9

Sleepers Awake

 Track 10

Gavottes I & II

from *Cello Suite No. 6*

 Track 11

Gavotte I
Allegretto

Track 12

Gavotte II

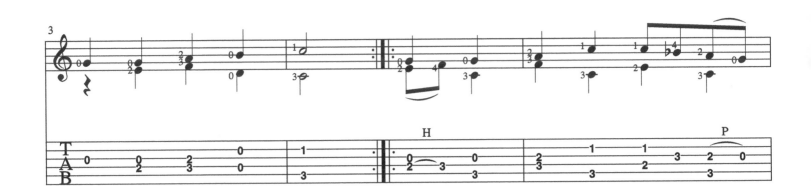

Track 13

D.C. al Gavotte I

Bourrée

from *Lute Suite No. 1*

 Track 14

Polacca

from *Brandenburg Concerto No. 1*

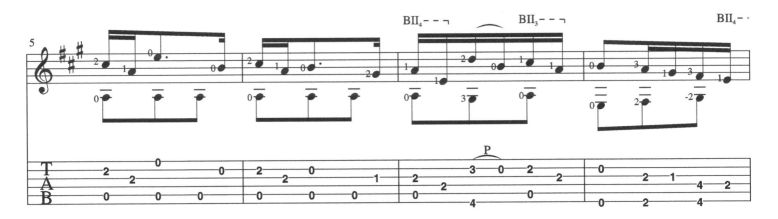

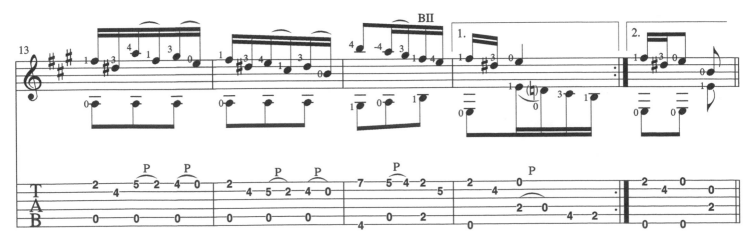

* ⌃ = *Staccatissimo.* Very short.

Menuet

from Cello Suite No. 2

 Track 16

Moderately

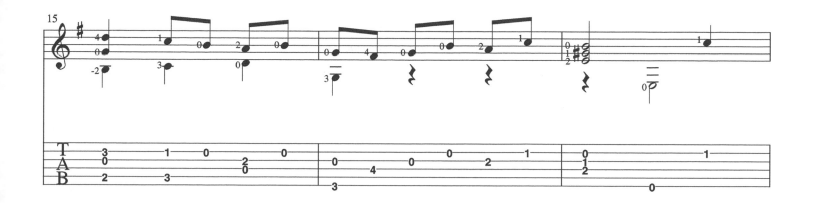

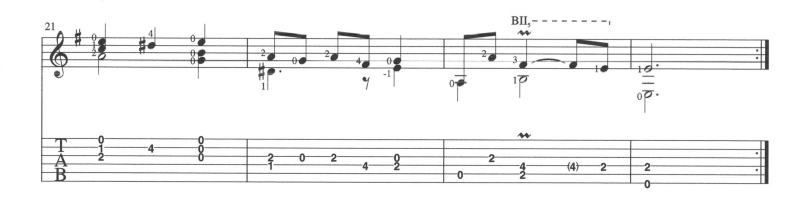

Gavottes I & II

from *Lute Suite No. 3*

 Track 17

Gavotte I
Allegretto

36

 Track 18

Gavotte II

Allegro

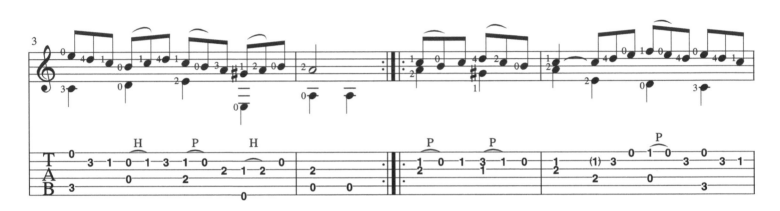

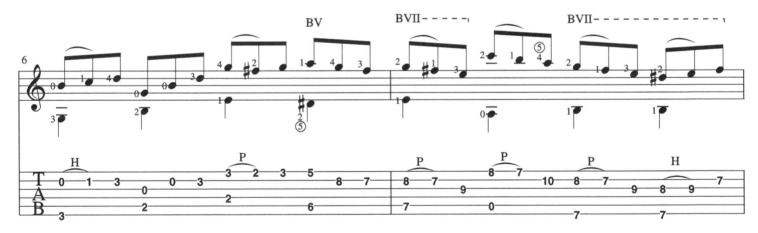

Prelude

(Little D Minor)

Track 19

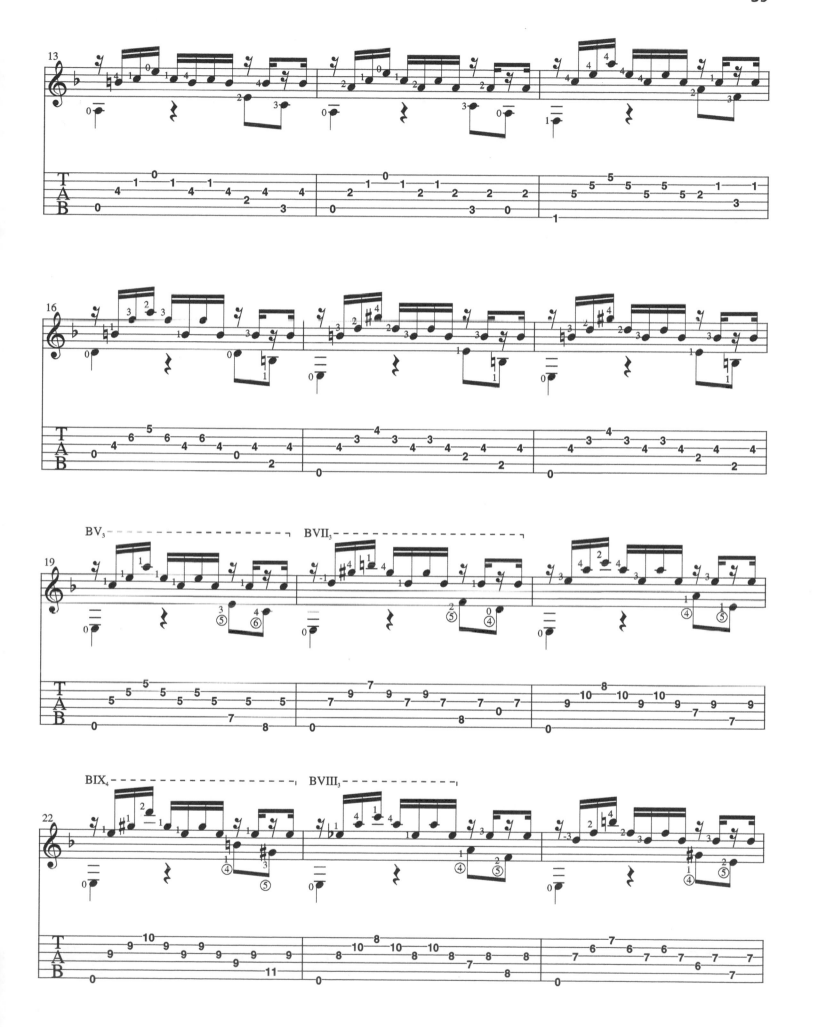

Air

from *Orchestral Suite III*

Track 20

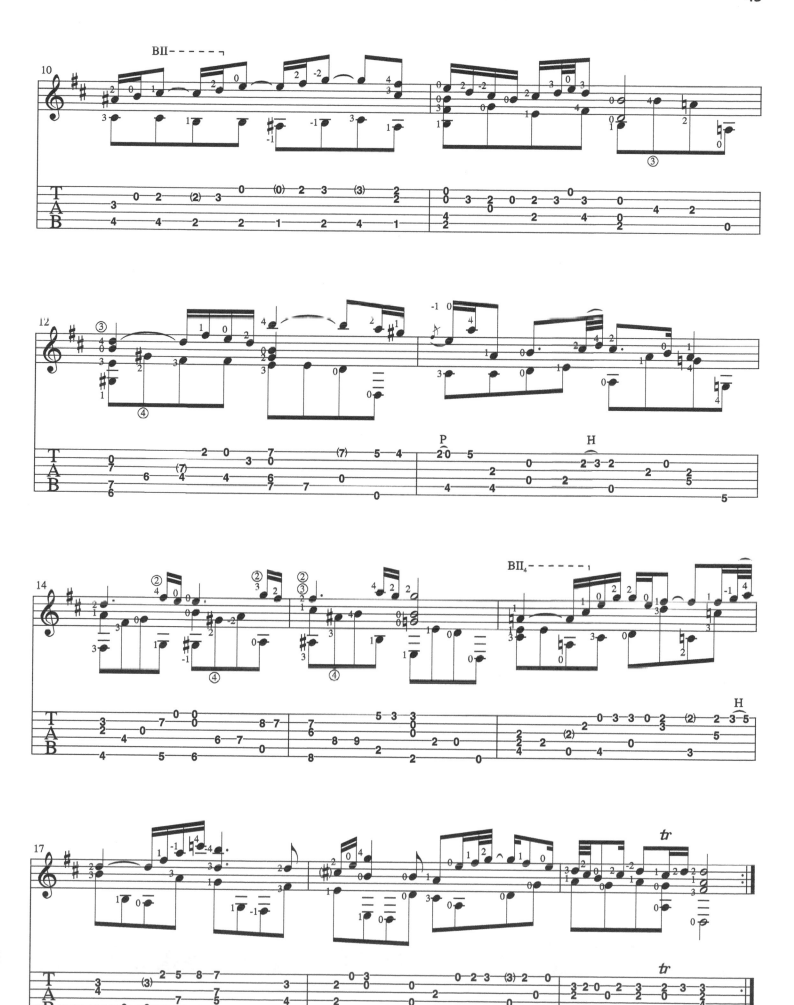